**At a Glance**™ Series — **DVD and Lesson Book**

T0061361

DVD Rock Bass

Written by Joe Charupakorn and Chad Johnson

Video Performers: Angeline Saris and Steven Hoffman

ISBN: 978-1-4803-0907-4

7777 W. BLUEMOUND RD. P.O. BOX 13819 MILWAUKEE, WI 53213

Visit Hal Leonard Online at
www.halleonard.com

TABLE OF CONTENTS

Introduction

Welcome to *DVD Rock Bass*, from Hal Leonard's exciting At a Glance series. Not as in-depth and slow moving as traditional method books, the material in *DVD Rock Bass* is presented in a snappy and fun manner and will help you start laying down some serious grooves in virtually no time at all. Plus, the At a Glance series uses real bass lines by real artists to illustrate how the concepts you're learning are used in the biggest hits of all time. For example, in *DVD Rock Bass*, you'll learn from rock classics like The Beatles' "Come Together," Pink Floyd's "Money," Ozzy Osbourne's "Crazy Train," and Cream's "Sunshine of Your Love," to name just a few.

Additionally, each book in the At a Glance series comes with a DVD containing video lessons that correspond to the printed material. The DVD that accompanies this book contains four video lessons, each approximately 8 to 10 minutes in length, that correspond to the topics covered in *DVD Rock Bass*. In these videos, ace instructors Angeline Saris and Steven Hoffman will show you in great detail the most important concepts you need to master to come up with killer bass lines. You'll learn about scales and how they're used in real songs—not just in theory—as well as the most common right-hand techniques used. Finally, you'll learn how to lock in with a kick drum and learn some essential must-know bass grooves. As you work through *DVD Rock Bass*, try to play the examples first on your own, and then check out the DVD for additional help or to see if you played it correctly. As the saying goes, "A picture is worth a thousand words," so be sure to use this invaluable tool on your quest to becoming the master of the low end.

ESSENTIAL ROCK BASS SCALES AND SHAPES

Nothing grooves like a good, solid bass line. And if you want to create your own memorable lines, it helps to know the raw materials and how they're applied to the fretboard. In this lesson, we'll learn the essential scales and fretboard shapes that have framed some of rock's most classic bass lines.

The Octave

Let's start with one of the most commonly used fretboard shapes of all: the octave. An *octave* is simply a higher or lower (in pitch) version of the same note. For example, the C note on string 1, fret 5 is one octave higher than the C note on string 3, fret 3. They sound the same, but one sounds higher (or lower) than the other.

Octave Shape 1

We're going to look at two different octave shapes on the bass fretboard. The first one is by far the most common and looks like this:

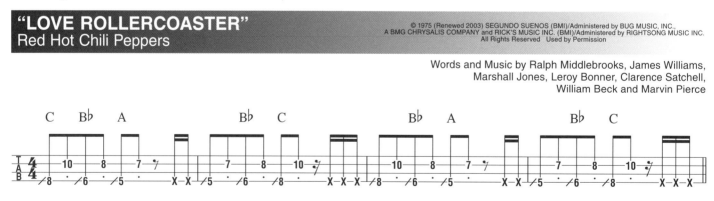

Those are G notes, but we could move this shape anywhere up and down this string set to play from a different root. The Red Hot Chili Peppers' "Love Rollercoaster" uses this octave shape first starting on a C root, played on string 4, fret 8 and string 2, fret 10. The riff moves backwards, going down to B♭ and A, all played on strings 4 and 2.

"LOVE ROLLERCOASTER"
Red Hot Chili Peppers

Words and Music by Ralph Middlebrooks, James Williams,
Marshall Jones, Leroy Bonner, Clarence Satchell,
William Beck and Marvin Pierce

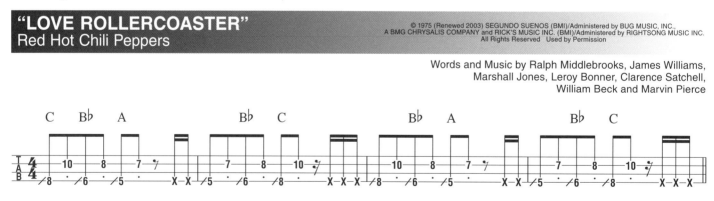

We can also move this shape up a string set to strings 3 and 1. If we play it in third position on those strings, we have C octaves:

4

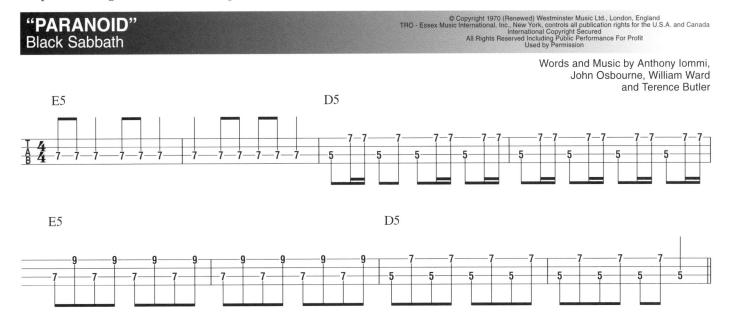

Black Sabbath's Geezer Butler uses the octave shape on strings 3 and 1 in "Paranoid." He starts out with the shape on string 3, fret 5 and string 2, fret 7, then moves it up two frets.

"PARANOID"
Black Sabbath

Words and Music by Anthony Iommi,
John Osbourne, William Ward
and Terence Butler

 It should be really easy to visualize the shape—two strings and two frets. You can come up with a pretty cool riff using nothing more than this shape. Just simply by messing with the two notes and some rhythms, you can easily get something like this:

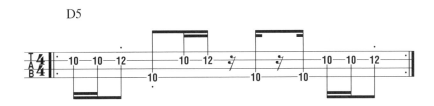

 Once you get the hang of the basic concept, it's easy to add other nearby notes as well. An easy one to add in is the ♭7th note, which is just a whole step below the root.

5

Octave Shape 2

The other, less common octave shape spans all four strings and uses the pinky on string 4. Here it is as a C octave in fifth position.

We don't use this one as much when moving back and forth between the low and high notes, but it creates a nice framework for other notes, which we'll look at in a bit.

The 5th

Another staple interval shape in the rock bassist's repertoire is the 5th—or the perfect 5th to be more specific. It's named a 5th because it represents the distance of five note names. For example, we say G to D is a 5th because five note names are involved between G to D:

$$G, \quad A, \quad B, \quad C, \quad \text{and} \quad D.$$
$$1, \quad 2, \quad 3, \quad 4, \quad \text{and} \quad 5$$

5th Shape 1

The most common 5th shape is similar to the octave shape in that there is a two-fret distance between the notes. However, rather than skipping a string as you did with the octave shape, 5ths are located on the adjacent string. If you've played any guitar, you may remember a 5th as the basis of a power chord shape. Here's a 5th from G to D on strings 4 and 3:

"Reach Out, I'll Be There" uses the 5th shape starting on fret 6 in measures 3–4.

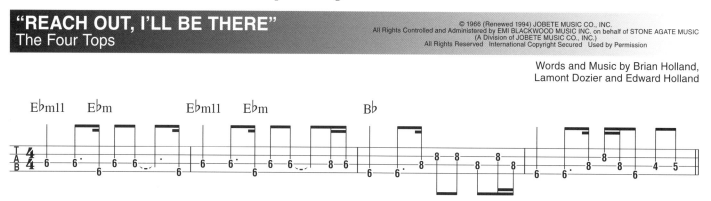

"REACH OUT, I'LL BE THERE"
The Four Tops

Words and Music by Brian Holland,
Lamont Dozier and Edward Holland

You can, of course, move the shape to the other remaining sets of adjacent strings—the 3/2 string set or the 2/1 string set—to play 5ths based off higher roots too:

The 5th is so strong that you can create a riff with just these two notes. The intro to "My Girl" is based solely on a 5th played on strings 3 and 2.

"MY GIRL"
The Temptations

Words and Music by William "Smokey" Robinson
and Ronald White

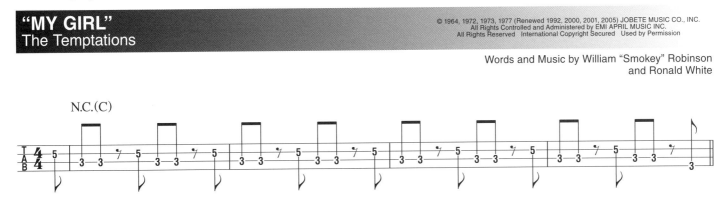

 Generally, the 5th is used to decorate the root note and add a bit of interest. You can add it to just about any root note in a rock tune, and it will usually sound good. Here's an example of how you might add the 5th to liven up a simple Bm–A–G progression. We're adding the 5th to the Bm and G chords on the way down and to the A chord on the way up. Notice how this example mixes up the 5ths; you don't necessarily have to play the root and 5th immediately after each other. You can mix it up however you like.

5th Shape 2

Similar to the second octave shape, our other 5th shape isn't used as often when playing with only the root and 5th, but again, it does outline a nice box shape for other notes and also can be helpful for visualizing the fretboard.

 Here is the shape as a 5th from A to E:

And of course you can move the shape to the 3/1 string set as well.

Minor Pentatonic Scale: 1–♭3–4–5–♭7

Ok, now let's check out some essential scales. Our first is the minor pentatonic, and it's been used to craft countless classic lines.

The minor pentatonic contains the root, ♭3rd, 4th, 5th, and ♭7th.

Minor Pentatonic Shape 1

Here's our first minor pentatonic shape, which is built off a fourth string root played with our first finger. We'll play it in fifth position for an A minor pentatonic scale.

Notice that our octave shape 1 is contained in this scale shape (E string, fret 5 and D string, fret 7).

Our 5th Shape 1 is also contained in this shape. Look closely and see if you can find it.

Minor Pentatonic Shape 2

The second minor pentatonic shape we'll look at contains the second octave shape (string 4, fret 5 and string 2, fret 2). We'll play in second position here for an A minor pentatonic scale.

Our 5th Shape 2 is also contained in this minor pentatonic shape. You should be able to easily see it.

Ok, so let's check out a few examples that use these shapes. Here's a line in A minor from shape 1, which puts us back in fifth position.

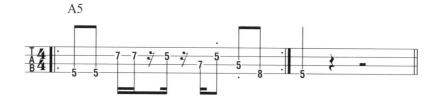

And here's one in C minor using shape 2, which keeps us in fifth position but uses a different box shape. This one's a bit funkier and busier. If you find the rhythms to be a little tricky, watch the slow demo on the DVD.

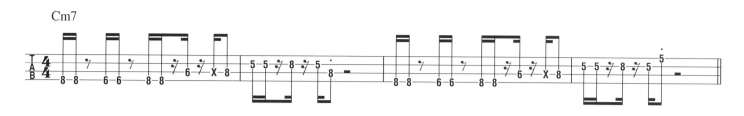

Of course, just because all of these notes are available doesn't mean you *have* to use every single one of them. In "You Really Got Me," Van Halen makes the most out of just two notes from Shape 2 of A minor pentatonic. In many cases, less is more.

"YOU REALLY GOT ME"
Van Halen

Words and Music by
Ray Davies

Tune Down 1/2 step:
(low to high) E♭–A♭–D♭–G♭

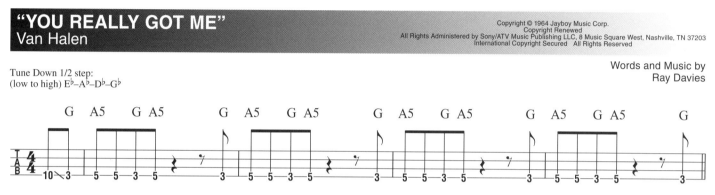

This "less is more" logic is also used in Rare Earth's "Get Ready," which is primarily built around just two notes of a Shape 2, D minor pentatonic scale, starting on string 3.

"GET READY"
Rare Earth

Words and Music by
William "Smokey" Robinson

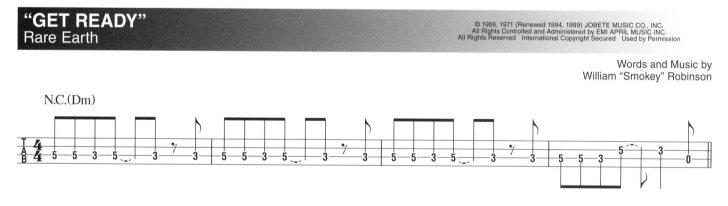

 ## Moving Between the Two Shapes

And here's an example of how we can combine the two shapes with a slide. We start off in Shape 2 but use a slide in measure 2 to move up to Shape 1.

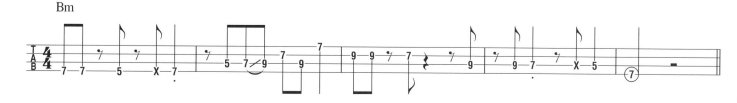

A good idea is to learn a few shapes for each minor pentatonic scale, so that you have several options always available. After you've completely mastered the shapes that we looked at, seek out a few more shapes either online, through some books, or through a teacher. With several shapes memorized and under your fingers, it's easy to create catchy bass lines.

Metallica joins together some E minor pentatonic shapes for a simple yet catchy riff in "Breadfan."

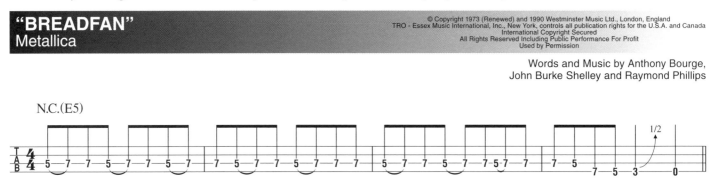

Blues Scale: 1–♭3–4–♭5–5–♭7

A close cousin of the minor pentatonic is the blues scale. The only difference is that we add one note: the ♭5th.

Blues Scale Shape 1

Let's change Shape 1 of our A minor pentatonic scale to a blues scale.

Blues Scale Shape 2

And here's how shape 2 would look. There are actually two different spots we could put the added ♭5th in this form. The optional one, which stretches out of position, is shown in parentheses.

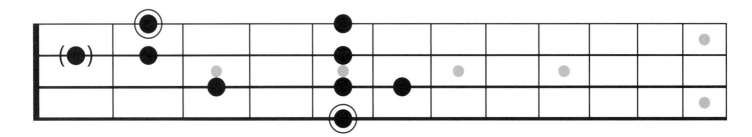

Let's check out the blues scale in action with a riff that would sound cool doubled by a guitar in a British blues-rock style. We're using Shape 1 of the A blues scale and adding some hammer-ons here.

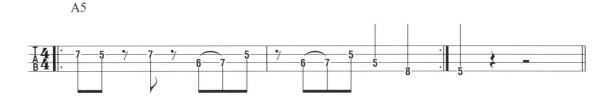

As suggested earlier, once you master these shapes, try learning a few more. Also learn some shapes that start with the root on a different string. The iconic blues scale lick in Black Sabbath's "Iron Man" is based on a B blues scale shape starting on string 3 with an added chromatic tone between the ♭7th and the root on the top.

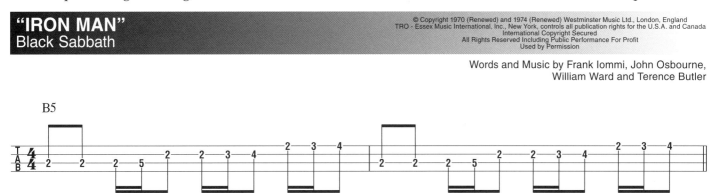

Tommy Shannon, of Stevie Ray Vaughan's Double Trouble, uses a variant on Shape 2 of the D blues scale (starting on string 3) as the basis for the riff in "Couldn't Stand the Weather."

Tune down 1/2 step:
(low to high) E♭–A♭–D♭–G♭

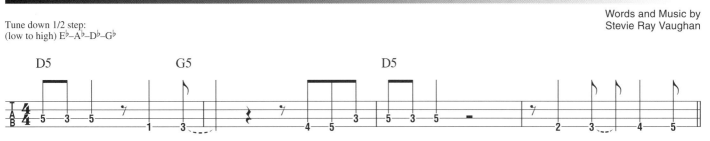

Cream's "Sunshine of Your Love" is the definition of the blues scale sound. This classic is based on the D blues scale combining shapes 1 and 2.

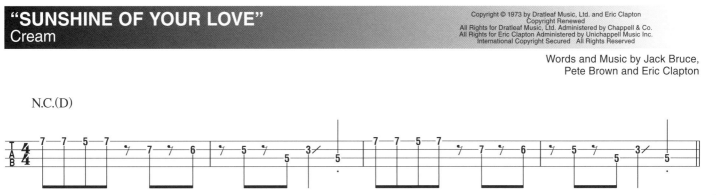

Major Pentatonic Scale: 1–2–3–5–6

Now let's check out the major pentatonic scale, which sounds upbeat and bright. It contains the root, 2nd, 3rd, 5th, and 6th.

Major Pentatonic Scale: Shape 1

There are countless shapes that you could learn but let's start with the most common shape, which we'll call Shape 1. Here's Shape 1 in the key of C, which puts us in seventh position.

Major Pentatonic Scale: Shape 2

Shape 2 of C major pentatonic puts us in fifth position. On this one, we'll add a low 6th, A, below the root.

Assuming you haven't fallen asleep, you probably noticed that C major pentatonic, Shape 2, looked exactly like A minor pentatonic, Shape 1. This wasn't a mistake. The two scales share exactly the same notes, because A minor is the relative minor of C major. The difference lies in how we treat the notes though. In the A minor pentatonic scale, A is the root, so our bass lines will be built as such. But in C major pentatonic, C is the root, and so it will get stressed more in the bass lines that we build from it.

The major pentatonic was used a lot in the old Motown style. Here's something in that vein using Shape 1 of D major pentatonic.

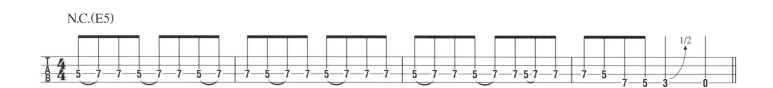

And here's a nice little groove in A using shape 2. Be careful not to rush the hammer-ons.

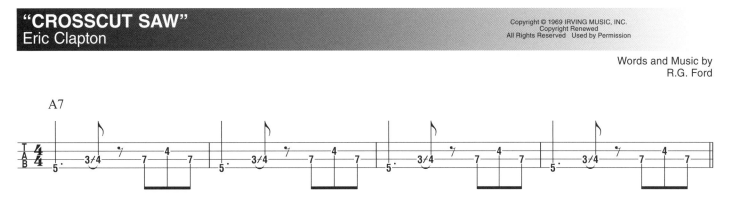

The bass line in Eric Clapton's version of "Crosscut Saw" is derived from a Shape 2, A major pentatonic scale.

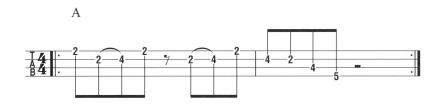

Words and Music by
R.G. Ford

Well that's gonna do it for this lesson. Between the octave, 5th, and the three scales we looked at, you've got the building blocks of thousands of bass lines in waiting. Enjoy putting these concepts to use!

ESSENTIAL ROCK BASS TECHNIQUE

Though the guitarists and singers often get the spotlight, the bass plays a powerful role in a rock band. Along with the drums, you make up half of the almighty rhythm section, which is the part of the music you feel as well as hear. In this lesson, we'll look at the essential techniques you need to play rock bass.

Right-Hand Technique

Let's start with the right hand, or left if you're left-handed—i.e., the plucking or picking hand. There are two main techniques used to pluck the strings: with the pick, or with the fingers.

Pick Style

Let's start with pick style. Most players usually prefer a fairly heavy pick for bass, such as a 1.2mm or thicker, but you should try a bunch out and see what feels best to you.

 On the DVD, the instructor Steven Hoffman is using a 1.2mm pick.

Grab the pick between your thumb and first finger, allowing a bit of the pointed end to protrude out. You may have to play around with the positioning a bit to find the perfect grip for your hand, but generally most players make contact between the tip and first joint of their first finger. The picking motion usually comes from the wrist. Watch the DVD to see what this looks like.

 Here's a short riff on strings 4 and 3 using all downstrokes. Be sure you're picking only one string at a time.

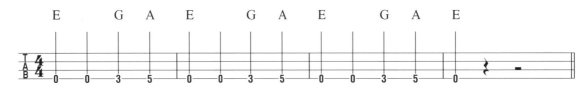

Adding Upstrokes

When you're playing notes that are a bit quicker, you'll want to add upstrokes for efficiency. This will take a bit of practice, but eventually it will feel as natural as the downstroke.

 Once you get comfortable with the feel of adding upstrokes, you can start adding in fretted notes. Here's a riff that alternates between only downstrokes and down–and–up strokes. You'll use the upstroke for the second of the two eighth notes played on beats 2 and 4.

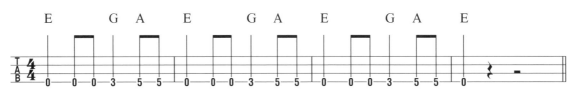

Let's now add upstrokes to notes that aren't just located on the low E string. Freddie King's "Hide Away" is based around fret 7 of string 3. Since this note is on an inner string, try not to accidentally hit string 4 when you use the upstroke.

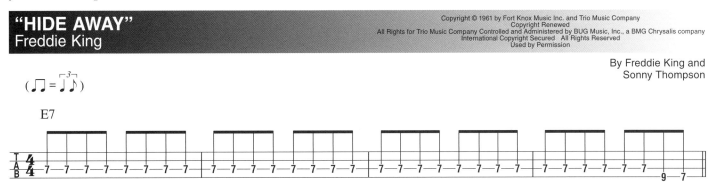

The Foo Fighters' "Monkey Wrench" uses strings 3 and 2. Again, be careful not to accidentally hit the surrounding open strings as you pick the bass line.

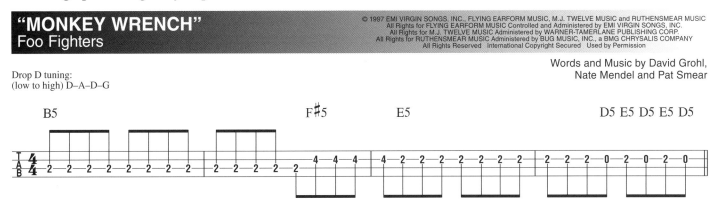

Palm Muting

Occasionally, you may want to choke or muffle the sound with a technique called *palm muting*. This is accomplished by laying your palm on the strings near the bridge as you pick. Watch the DVD to first hear how the E string sounds normally then how it sounds with the palm mute applied. The farther you move in from the bridge, the more muted it sounds.

Let's check out the sound of palm muting in another bass line. The symbol "P.M. Throughout" tells you to apply the palm mute through the whole phrase. This one's in the key of G.

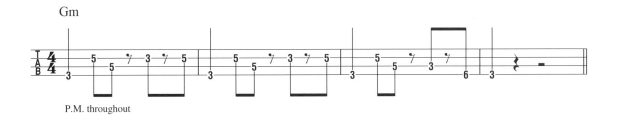

Use palm muting to get the staccato sound on Eric Clapton's "Lay Down Sally."

"LAY DOWN SALLY"
Eric Clapton

Words and Music by Eric Clapton,
Marcy Levy and George Terry

P.M. throughout

Alternate Picking

For fast, 16th-note lines, you'll need to employ alternate picking when playing with a pick. This means alternating down and upstrokes continuously, like the instructor does on the DVD.

Let's start with Filter's "Hey Man Nice Shot," which isn't impossibly fast and has all the notes contained on the low E string.

"HEY MAN NICE SHOT"
Filter

Words and Music by
Richard Patrick

Drop D tuning:
(low to high) D–A–D–G

N.C.

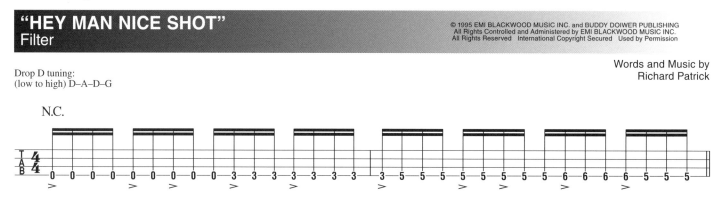

Syncopation

In many musical situations, however, you won't be picking continuous 16th notes, as rhythms are often a bit more varied than that. Even if you play a phrase that has a lot of rests or ties, it's still important to get into the habit of pairing downstrokes with downbeats and upstrokes with upbeats. This will allow you to pick intricate rhythms without having to think too much about it—the correct stroke will become instinctive.

⊓ = downstroke

V = upstroke

In this riff, you might notice that, from beats 1 to 2, there are two downstrokes and two upstrokes in a row—that's not randomly done. The strokes coincide with which part of the beat the note falls on. In a 16th-note based phrase like this, the first and third 16ths are played with downstrokes, and the second and fourth 16ths are played with upstrokes. In general, your hand should be sort of continuously moving, with your pick only making contact with the string when it needs to. If you're confused, the DVD also demonstrates the phrase played a little slower so you can see the picking.

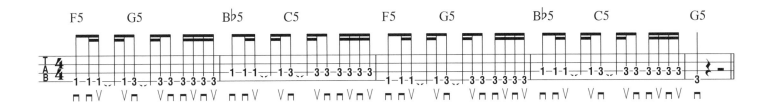

Fingerstyle

The other method for plucking strings is fingerstyle. This results in a slightly mellower sound, but it's an extremely versatile technique that's used by players in all genres, including rock.

The first and second fingers are most often used for plucking, and the motion involves simply dragging or rolling the finger across the string. Watch the DVD to see this demonstrated.

Resting the Thumb

When you're plucking the E string, you can rest your thumb on the pickup. But when you're plucking any other string, the thumb should rest on the E string to keep it quiet. Your plucking fingers should follow through and come to rest on the next string. This also aids in keeping unwanted string noise out.

Alternating Fingers

When playing notes at moderate or quick tempos, it's most efficient to alternate between the first and second finger. Instead of picking this eighth-note line with only the first finger, it's much easier to alternate between the first and second finger.

Raking or "Dragging"

There is an exception to this alternating fingers rule, though. When crossing from a thinner to a thicker string, such as from string 2 to 3, we use the same plucking finger to simply rake through both strings with one smooth motion.

Instead of picking these four notes with alternating fingers, for example, we'll rake from string 2 to string 3 with one smooth stroke. Watch the DVD here to see what that looks like.

Here's an example that puts these concepts to work. We'll use alternate plucking fingers for the most part but will rake when we cross strings.

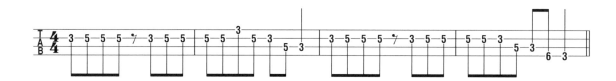

Left-Hand Techniques

Let's check out a few left-hand techniques that no good rock bassist should be without.

Slides

The first technique we'll look at is the *slide*. This is a self-explanatory move that involves sliding a fret-hand finger up or down the fretboard while maintaining contact with the string.

Slides can be very precise, where we target specific notes, or imprecise, where they're used more for effect. They can also be slurred or plucked. Let's check out some examples.

Here are some plucked slides with specific target notes.

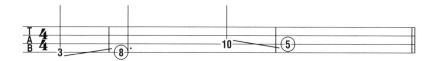

Or we can play that same thing using slurred slides, in which case the second note is not plucked. It's just sounded by the sliding motion.

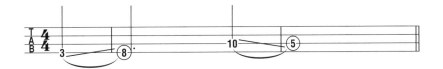

It's also common to slide up into a target note from a non-specific distance—usually a few frets, but it can be more drastic too and adds a great deal of character without adding too much work. These are *grace-note slides* and don't take up any real rhythmic time.

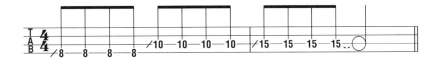

Let's take a look at a few examples using different types of slides. Here's a Motown-influenced line that uses ascending and descending slurred slides. This one might be a little tricky at first, so start slowly if you need to. Notice how the slide allows us to smoothly shift into a higher position. This is something that's often exploited in lines that travel around the fretboard.

And here's an example where long, drawn-out slides are emphasized for effect. Make the slides slow and deliberate.

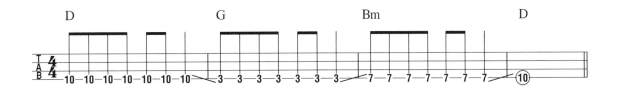

The slides in The Beatles' "Come Together" really give the song its signature sound.

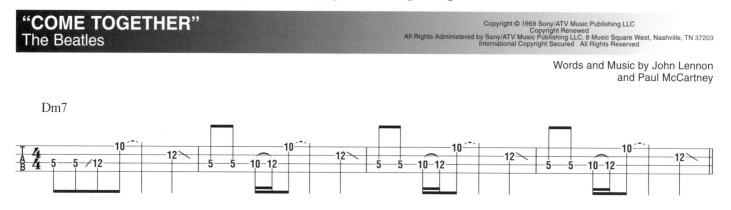

Hammer-Ons and Pull-Offs

Now let's take a look at *hammer-ons* and *pull-offs*, which are also extremely popular. Both techniques involve plucking one note and then using the left hand only to sound the next note.

To execute a hammer-on, you pluck the first note and then use another finger of the fret hand to "hammer" down onto a higher fret on the same string. Here, you only pluck the fifth-fret notes and then hammer on to the seventh-fret notes.

The bass line for Ozzy Osbourne's "No More Tears" incorporates hammer-ons alternating against an open D string.

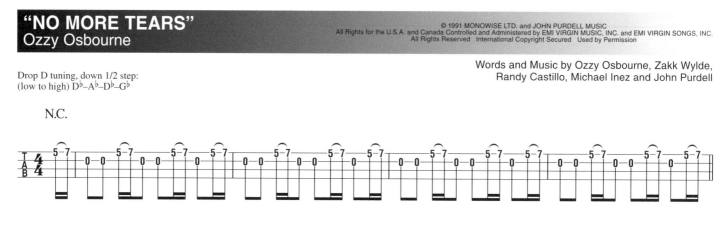

Of course, you can also hammer a note from an open string.

The pull-off is kind of the opposite of a hammer-on, but it's a bit more difficult because it requires a little preparation. You'll need to fret both notes—the higher one and lower one—at the same time. You pluck the higher one and then pull that fret-hand finger down and off the string, essentially plucking the string to sound the lower note.

In this example, you pick the seventh fret notes but keep the fifth fret notes planted as well, pulling off into them after the seventh fret notes are sounded.

As with the hammers, you can also pull off to an open string:

The bass line to Rod Stewart's "Maggie May" uses pull-offs to both fretted notes and to an open string.

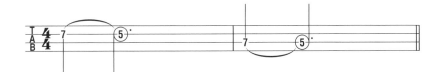

Words and Music by Rod Stewart
and Martin Quittenton

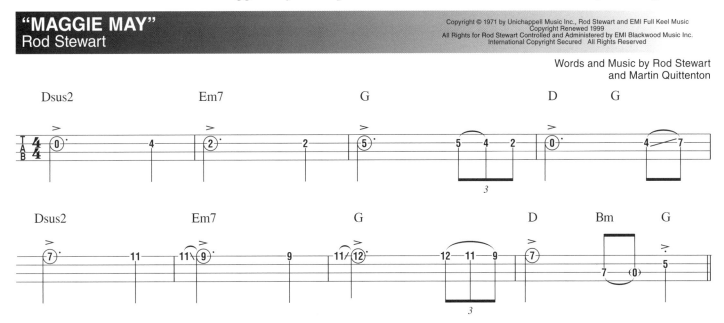

Hammer-ons and pull-offs can help make it easier to play quicker lines, but they're also used for the smooth sound they create. Let's close out this lesson with an example that makes liberal use of both. Watch the DVD to also hear this example played slowly.

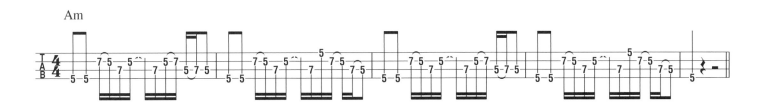

Well that'll wrap it up. You should now be equipped with the techniques to tackle most rock bass lines. It's just a matter of practice, practice, practice from here on out. Good luck!

LOCKING IN WITH THE KICK DRUM

As a bassist, you're an integral part of the rhythm section. Therefore, it's extremely important for you to be in sync with the drums—with regards to both tempo and style. One of the most tried-and-true methods to assure this is happening is by locking in with the kick drum. In this lesson, we'll learn how to make things really thump by teaming up with your drummer's foot.

The Importance of Listening

Though we, as musicians, are the ones playing the music, it's just as important, if not more so, to spend a good time *listening* as well. This holds true for any musician. Often times, the biggest difference between a below-average player and one that's considered great is the simple fact that one has spent time developing his ear, while the other has not.

You could spend years practicing to play some pretty impressive stuff. But if you never bother to actually listen to what you're playing and/or listen to others that you're playing with, you're selling yourself short, big-time. With regards to this lesson, we're talking about listening to the drummer—specifically the kick drum.

The Four-Beat Pattern

Many typical kick drum patterns last four beats, or one measure. This isn't to say that they'll repeat the same thing every time; it's just that the basic feel is usually established over the course of one measure. Let's take a look at some of the more common ones.

Kick Pattern 1

Let's illustrate this by starting with probably the most basic beat of all.

There is no syncopation at all; it's played on beats 1, 3, and 3.5 only. This tells us that we need a bass line that doesn't syncopate much. It should be driving and straightforward. Maybe something like this line in A.

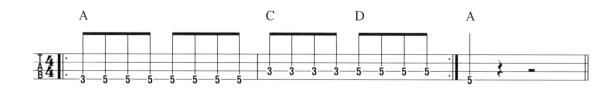

That's almost as straightforward as it gets. All we did was add a G note "push" before the A to give it a little boot. Blink 182's "What's My Age Again?" pumps away at straight eighth notes.

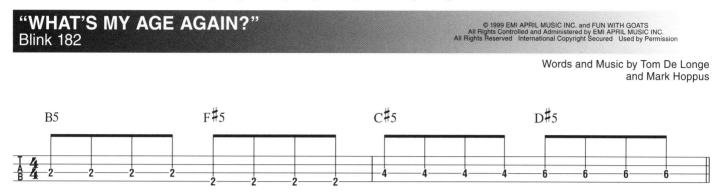

Words and Music by Tom De Longe
and Mark Hoppus

Notice that I said we need a line that doesn't syncopate much. However, we still have a little leeway with even this kick pattern, because it does hit on the "and" of beat 3. So we could accent that eighth note and still not be working against the drums. Here's how that might sound. The main thing is that the bass part has to work *with*, and not against the music.

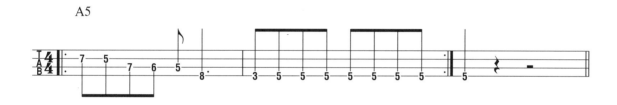

Kick Pattern 2

Ok, let's check out another kick pattern. This one is still all eighth-note based, but it introduces a common syncopation. We're accenting the "and" of beat 2 here. The "and" of beat 3 is hit as well, but this one doesn't stick out as much because it's quickly followed by the snare on beat 4, so it sounds more like a pickup into that beat.

The "and" of beat 2 can't be ignored, however. We really need to hit that with the kick in order to make the rhythm section sound like one unit. So we might play something like this in C. Do you see where the accents of the line fall?

The Police's hit, "Message in a Bottle," also exploits these accents.

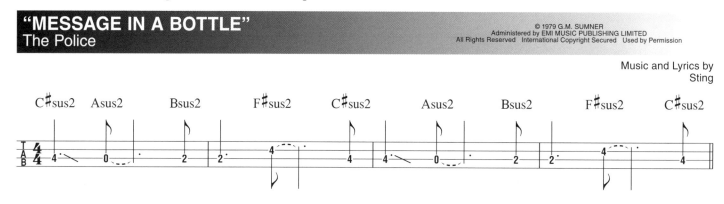

Music and Lyrics by
Sting

We can take a bit more liberty with it as well, as long as we don't step on that crucial syncopation by accenting beat 2 instead of the "and," and throwing off the rhythm. For example, we could accent the "and" of beats 1, 2, and 3 and still fall in line with the drums. Here's an example of that in the key of G.

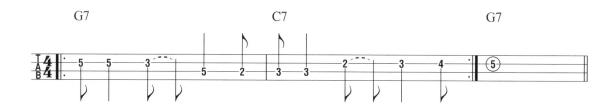

Kick Pattern 3

All right, now let's check out a beat that brings a 16th-note syncopation into play.

You can hear that the tempo is a bit slower on this one. That's the norm for a beat that syncopates 16th notes. Obviously, the big deal here is the "a" of beat 2—the last 16th note in that beat. Again, the "and" of beat 3 is also played, but that's more in prep of the following snare on beat 4. So the critical thing here is accenting that last 16th in beat 2, which tends to sound a little funkier.

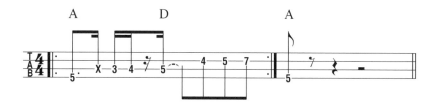

We don't have to play a busy line either. We could leave a lot of space and play only on the kick drum beats for an entirely different effect. It's simple but very effective.

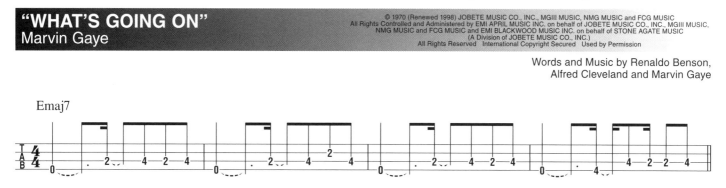

This type of figure can be heard in soul and R&B classics like Marvin Gaye's "What's Going On."

Words and Music by Renaldo Benson,
Alfred Cleveland and Marvin Gaye

Kick Pattern 4

Let's look at one more pattern that adds another 16th-note syncopation: This one is definitely the least common so far, but we're looking at it because it adds a legitimately different syncopation: the "e" of beat 3. Obviously, there are lots more kick patterns possible, but many of them simply add a note here and there without changing the basic feel of the first three patterns we looked at. This one changes it significantly.

We have the "a" of beat 1 and the "e" of beat 3. The "a" of beat 1 doesn't stand out as much because of the following snare, but the "e" of beat 3 is loud and proud. So we want to hit that.

And now let's try another one that uses much more space. We're only playing one more note than the kick pattern here.

So you can see that we have a wide range of possibilities while still reinforcing the kick's rhythm. That does is for this lesson. I hope you've gained some respect for the power of a unified rhythm section. It really feels great to lock in with a drummer in this way. Good luck!

MUST-KNOW BASS GROOVES

Music is a language, and just as there are words and phrases in the English language we must know in order to function in society, there are musical concepts and phrases essential to functioning as a working musician. The bass is no exception. If you want to get gigs as a bassist, there are some stock grooves that you simply must know, because they'll show up time and time again. And that's what this lesson is all about.

While it's impossible in our limited time to get too specific with regards to individual bass lines, we'll focus more on concepts and demonstrate each with a typical bass line.

Steady Eighth Notes

The first concept we'll look at is the steady eighth-note line. This is something that's been used by everyone from U2 to Tom Petty to Sting to the Red Hot Chili Peppers. The idea is to provide a steady, almost hypnotic pulse of eighth notes on roots that effortlessly propels the music. Repeated notes—rather than quickly moving lines—tend to be the order of the day with this approach. Here's a simple idea in E.

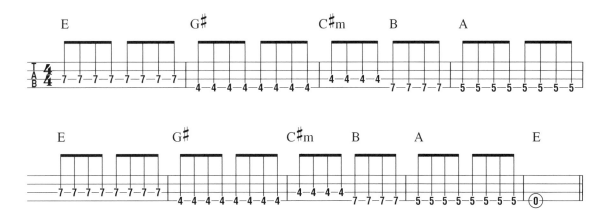

The Who's "I Can See for Miles" makes use of steady eighth notes to power its engine.

"I CAN SEE FOR MILES"
The Who

Words and Music by
Peter Townshend

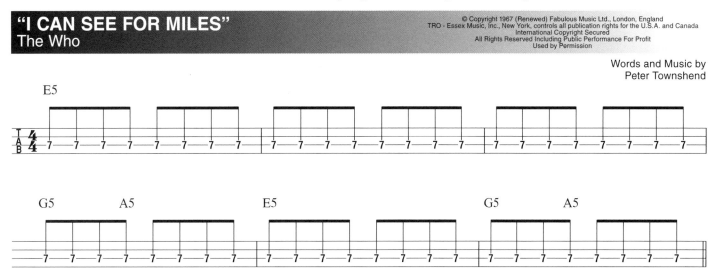

Two things are really important here: timing and consistency of volume. If either one of those wanders consistently, the groove will suffer big time. Both of these things might not seem like a big deal on the surface, but in reality, they are the most important factors in making things sound good. No matter how many scales or patterns you know, if you can't play them with a steady pulse, or your playing sounds unintentionally uneven, you're going to have a very difficult time getting called to play bass on a good gig.

Dominant Arpeggios

Another big staple, especially in blues rock and older rock 'n' roll, is the dominant seventh arpeggio line. You'll hear this all over the place in those styles. There are endless variations on this, but suffice it to say that you need to learn a few ways to finger dominant arpeggios so you can whip them out in any key at a moment's notice.

Here's a typical idea in A that shows two common patterns: one for the I chord, A7, and another for the IV chord, D7.

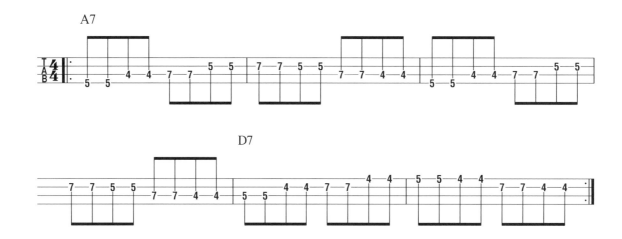

So for the A7, we're using only the notes from an A7 arpeggio.

For the D7, though, we're using a slight variation. Instead of just playing root, 3rd, 5th, ♭7th, root, we're playing root, 3rd, 5th, 6th, ♭7th. The basic shape and sound of both arpeggios are similar enough to make it all sound connected. You can mix and match these ideas throughout if you want to keep things interesting.

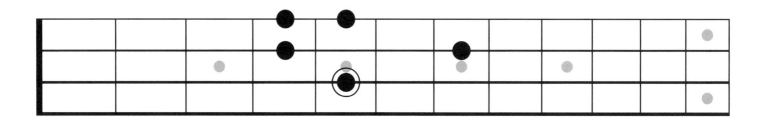

An E7 arpeggio serves as the basis for "Crossfire," as played by Stevie Ray Vaughan.

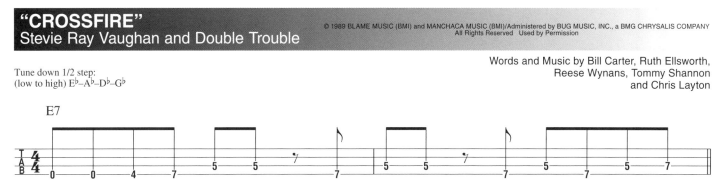

"CROSSFIRE"
Stevie Ray Vaughan and Double Trouble

Words and Music by Bill Carter, Ruth Ellsworth,
Reese Wynans, Tommy Shannon
and Chris Layton

Tune down 1/2 step:
(low to high) E♭–A♭–D♭–G♭

Descending Scale Pattern

The next device we'll look at is the descending scale bass line. This is most often used with a chord progression that uses inversions so that the bass line descends straight down the major scale. The Beatles used this a lot, but it appears everywhere, really.

As long as you know some major scale fingerings, this one should be easy to implement once you recognize it. Here's a typical example in D. Note that this example is using a mix of different rhythms. Just because we're using descending scale patterns, you shouldn't automatically assume that they are going to be fast, virtuosic scale runs.

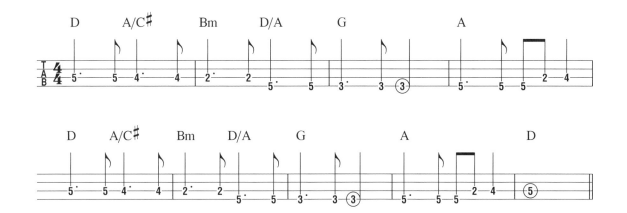

The bass figure during the guitar solo in Ozzy Osbourne's "Crazy Train" takes a ride down an F♯ minor scale.

"CRAZY TRAIN"
Ozzy Osbourne

Words and Music by Ozzy Osbourne,
Randy Rhoads and Bob Daisley

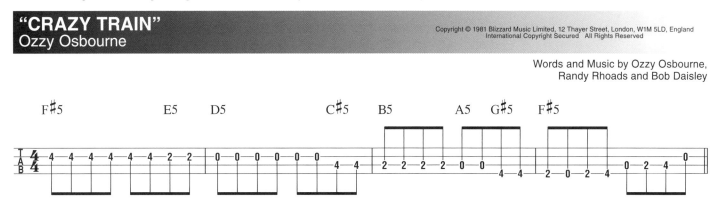

There are many variations on this. Sometimes a chromatic note may be interjected in between two other scale tones. The bass figure for the intro to Aerosmith's "Dream On" makes subtle use of chromatics to add to its moody feel.

"DREAM ON"
Aerosmith

Words and Music by
Steven Tyler

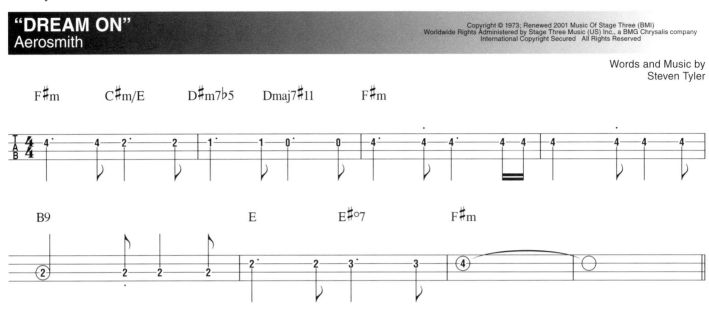

Repetitive Minor Pentatonic Riffs

Here's an idea you see in a lot of British rock: the repetitive minor pentatonic riff. Most repetitive minor pentatonic riffs are catchy, and it's a pretty common concept. You'll need to have plenty of variations on this type of thing in your arsenal.

Here's an idea in G.

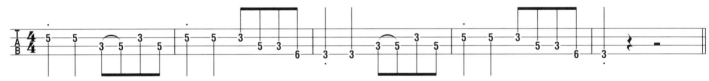

This whole riff came out of a G minor pentatonic scale form right here in third position.

Root-5th-Octave

Next we'll look at the root-5th-octave move. This is sort of a combination of several moves, such as root-5th and root-octave. Suffice it to say that the root, 5th, and octave will get you by in many situations.

Here's an example in B minor. In this example, a few of the notes are syncopated, which helps give the rhythm a shot of adrenalin now and then.

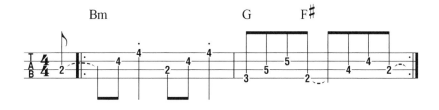

That same B minor starting point serves as the foundation for the bass line in Pink Floyd's "Money."

"MONEY"
Pink Floyd

Words and Music by
Roger Waters

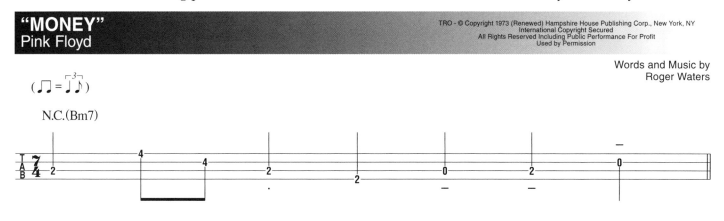

Major Pentatonic Riffs

You'll also hear your fair share of major pentatonic riffs—particularly using a sliding scale form. For E major pentatonic, for example, we'd play this form.

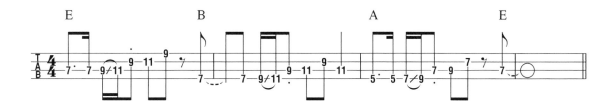

And here's an example in E of how we might move this scale form around in a tune. This one has a lot of motion.

Queen's "Crazy Little Thing Called Love" uses the D major pentatonic as the basis of its bouncy groove.

Growling, Grungy Blues Scale Lines

You can get a really powerful sound by working in a bass ostinato using the blues scale—just ask Alice in Chains, Soundgarden, and a host of other hard grunge rockers.

 It's common to use the lowest open note as the root, so we'll play a demonstrative line here from the E blues scale. Only a few notes and a low E, and you have a beast of a line.

 The idea here is to work off the blues scale entirely on the bottom string for a really thick, meaty sound. Here's how the E blues scale looks when played on string 4 entirely. It's easy to come up with bass lines with the notes organized this way. This idea is used in drop D tuning a lot as well. Of course, you'd then be playing a D blues scale, but the shape would look the same.

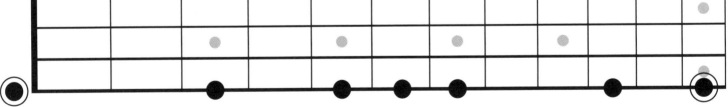

You can also use the pick to get some extra clicking noise in more active grooves. Watch the DVD to see and hear how it's done.

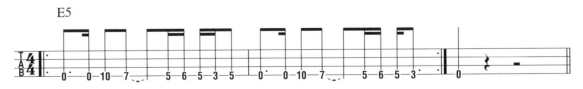

Well, that'll wrap it up. Granted, we've only really scratched the surface here, but if you spend some time with these concepts and work out a few variations of each, you'll be armed with the skills to quickly tackle a large percentage of the lines that come your way. Good luck, and enjoy the journey!